Father God, After Believing in Jesus as Savior, Can One

LOSE THEIR SALVATION?

RICK WILSON

About the Author

I am the eldest son of a pastor. Raised in a very conservative home, I accepted Jesus as Savior at a very early age; but before I graduated high school, I became a father, got married, and got divorced! That was just the beginning. I lived a life that included five failed marriages and knew no out of bounds in those marriages. Drugs, alcohol, and insane behavior were the norm.

Over the years I walked with Jesus for brief times. Those times were usually a result of hitting a rock bottom. However, Jesus always responded to my cries for help. Jesus never said no! I was the unfaithful one whose heart was prone to wander, just like the old Baptist hymn says, my flesh was stronger than I was.

When I was in my late forties and not walking with Jesus, the questions came. How could a God of justice still have love and mercy for someone like me—someone who was unfaithful and evil by any standard? The Ten Commandments weren't even recommendations to me.

I was someone who was unlovable; even I couldn't stand to be around myself. What's worse than self-hate? Yet at my last rock bottom, at the age of fifty, homeless and living out of my car, I cried out again and Jesus rescued me...again. He still loved me. In time, I met and married a strong woman of God. The only marriage founded in Christ Jesus.

Jesus is still answering questions in the book of my life, and this book is one.

It was quoted by the celebrated author Leo Tolstoy,

> The most difficult subjects can be explained to the most slow-witted man if he has not formed any idea of them already; but the simplest thing cannot be made clear to the most intelligent man if he is firmly persuaded that he knows already, without a shadow of doubt, what is laid before him.

I bear witness to Mr. Tolstoy's quote regarding one losing their salvation until I found out that I was overwhelmingly wrong. I had believed a lie.

That being said, the purpose of this writing is to address the very controversial question: Once one has believed in Jesus as Lord of their life, can they lose their salvation?

Father God, we ask for Your wisdom in answering the questions presented in our lives. In Jesus name Amen.

We will look at scriptures pertaining to God's definition of sin(s), and it's consequences in both the old and new covenants. We will compare high lights of each covenant. We will explore how both covenants often intertwine bringing heavy burdens (guilt/shame) or grateful release from these burdens. And these questions will provoke frequently asked questions which will be addressed later.

Even though I am a son of a pastor, raised in a Christian home and was born again at a young age; I ran hard from God for most of my adult life, until the age of fifty. Many would say that if I had died in these dark and sin filled seasons of my life that I would be in hell and I believed this of myself.

ISBN 978-1-0980-3650-8 (paperback)
ISBN 978-1-0980-3651-5 (digital)

Christian Faith Publishing, Inc.
832 Park Avenue
Meadville, PA 16335
www.christianfaithpublishing.com

Printed in the United States of America

PART 1

To add relevance to this topic, let's first look at the extremes that God will go through to give a single person eternal life with Him. This is also an indication of the lengths He will go to, to bring back a prodigal (rebellious) child.

We all know John 3:16 (NLT):

> For this is how God loved the world: He gave his one and only Son, so that everyone who believes in him will not perish but have eternal life.

So anyone who believes in Jesus will be saved, period.

This kind of belief is absolute. We believers stake our salvation on this verse, and it is true because Jesus (the only sacrifice required by Father God for our sins) said so. God's sacrifice of His one and only Son is the only scriptural sacrifice God required under the new covenant for the atonement (or forgiveness) of sin.

But how far will God go for one person? Undoubtedly, we all know a person or persons who do not yet believe in Jesus. We also know that God never stops seeking those who are lost so they may be found.

> A mob quickly formed against Paul and Silas, and the city officials ordered them stripped and beaten with wooden rods. They were severely beaten, and then they were thrown into prison. The jailer was ordered to make sure they didn't escape. So the jailer put them into the inner dungeon and clamped their feet in the stocks.

> Around midnight Paul and Silas were praying and singing hymns to God, and the other prisoners were listening. Suddenly, there was a massive earthquake, and the prison was shaken to its foundations. All the doors immediately flew open, and the chains of every prisoner fell off! The jailer woke up to see the prison doors wide open. He assumed the prisoners had escaped, so he drew his sword to kill himself. But Paul shouted to him, "Stop! Don't kill yourself! We are all here!"
>
> The jailer called for lights and ran to the dungeon and fell down trembling before Paul and Silas. Then he brought them out and asked, "Sirs, what must I do to be saved?"
>
> They replied, "Believe in the Lord Jesus and you will be saved, along with everyone in your household." And they shared the word of the Lord with him and with all who lived in his household. (Acts 16:22–32, NLT)

So God allowed Paul and Silas to be severely beaten with rods and imprisoned. God made an earthquake to open the doors to a prison to get Paul and Silas out and stopped the jailer from committing suicide so that jailer would believe in Jesus and be saved. Then God saved the man's family. What manner of love is this that God would go to these extremes as well as sacrificing His one and only Son to make the whole process possible?

For those of us with children and grandchildren who are walking in the world *without* believing in Jesus, know this:

> Many will come from you. I will make nations of you. Kings will come from you. I will make My agreement between Me and you and your children after you through their whole lives for all time. I will be God to you and to your children's children after you. (Gen. 17:6–7, NLV)

6

FATHER GOD, AFTER BELIEVING IN JESUS AS SAVIOR, CAN ONE LOSE THEIR SALVATION?

In these scriptures, God is talking to Abraham. Abraham was also under a grace covenant. This scripture happened about four hundred years before the Law of Moses. It was at this time that God made this promise to all of Abraham's children, which includes us who have believed in Jesus today. I am saying this so when you look at your children or grandchildren and don't see them walking with Jesus at this moment, *don't worry. Their earthquake is coming! Their chains of bondage will drop off! The door to their imprisoned, hard hearts will be opened, and they will believe in the Son of the Living God, King Jesus, and they will be saved!*

The extremes God will go to, to save a single person are well-documented with a specific promise for our families.

If your children or grandchildren are saved and have walked away from God as I did, see part 2.

PART 2

The New Covenant's Perfection through the Sacrifice of Jesus

Luke 22:20 (NKJV) says, "Likewise He also took the cup after supper, saying, 'This cup is the new covenant in My blood, which is shed for you.'"

Now let's see what God's Word has to say about His view on sin and righteousness. Also, we'll look at His view of those who have believed in Jesus as Lord under the only covenant in which believers after the resurrection of Jesus are under: the new covenant.

> And the result of God's gracious gift is very different from the result of that one man's sin. For Adam's sin led to condemnation, but God's free gift leads to our being made right with God, even though we are guilty of many sins. For the sin of this one man, Adam, caused death to rule over many. But even greater is God's wonderful grace and his gift of righteousness, for all who receive it will live in triumph over sin and death through this one man, Jesus Christ.
>
> Yes, Adam's one sin brings condemnation for everyone, but Christ's one act of righteousness brings a right relationship with God and new life for everyone. Because one-person dis-

obeyed God, many became sinners. But because one other person obeyed God, many will be made righteous.

God's law was given so that all people could see how sinful they were. But as people sinned more and more, God's wonderful grace became more abundant. So just as sin ruled over all people and brought them to death, now God's wonderful grace rules instead, giving us right standing with God and resulting in eternal life through Jesus Christ our Lord. (Rom. 5:16–21, NLT)

In verse 16, we are right with God, even though we are guilty of many sins. This is in present tense, not past tense. In other words, we are right with God, even though we continue, to sin because of the grace of God through Christ Jesus!

Another one of the real significances of the above scriptures is the fact that we are born a sinner. Most people are taught that we are sinners because we sin. We are sinners because Adam sinned. It's our DNA as being in the linage of Adam (human beings). That is why we must be born again.

There was a man named Nicodemus, a Jewish religious leader who was a Pharisee. After dark one evening, he came to speak with Jesus. "Rabbi," he said, "we all know that God has sent you to teach us. Your miraculous signs are evidence that God is with you."

Jesus replied, "I tell you the truth, unless you are born again, you cannot see the Kingdom of God."

"What do you mean?" exclaimed Nicodemus. "How can an old man go back into his mother's womb and be born again?"

Jesus replied, "I assure you, no one can enter the Kingdom of God without being born of water and the Spirit. 6 Humans can reproduce only human life, but the Holy Spirit gives birth to spiritual life. (John 3:1–6, NLT)

The birth of the Spirit and water (or to be born again) is a birth that takes us to places and locations that are out of our reach and control. We still have the soul in our possession, which is made up of our mind, will, and emotions. But the spirit man is out of reach. The moment we are born again, our spirit man is seated in heavenly places. We are at that moment a new creature in a new place.

Therefore, if anyone is in Christ, he is a new creation; old things have passed away; behold, all things have become new. Now all things are of God, who has reconciled us to Himself through Jesus Christ, and has given us the ministry of reconciliation, that is, that God was in Christ reconciling the world to Himself, not imputing their trespasses to them, and has committed to us the word of reconciliation. (2 Cor. 5:17–19, NKJV)

That even though we were dead because of our sins, he gave us life when he raised Christ from the dead. (It is only by God's grace that you have been saved!) For he raised us from the dead along with Christ and seated us with him in the heavenly realms because we are united with Christ Jesus. So God can point to us in all future ages as examples of the incredible wealth of his grace and kindness toward us, as shown in all he has done for us who are united with Christ Jesus. (Eph. 2:5–7, NLT)

But the person who is joined to the Lord is one spirit with him. (1 Cor. 6:17, NLT)

FATHER GOD, AFTER BELIEVING IN JESUS AS SAVIOR, CAN ONE LOSE THEIR SALVATION?

Once we are a new creature in Christ Jesus and seated in heavenly places with Him, that location is unchangeable by the future choices of our free will. Abba Father and King Jesus will not allow changes in the spirit realms of heaven or hell. At salvation we believed in Him, and He forgave us of our sins. From that point in time He remembers our sins no more, even as we commit them. Jesus died for all our sins past, present, and future. At the time of His death, all our sins were future sins because we weren't born yet, and we stand before God without a single fault from the point of salvation through all eternity. Once we are born again, we are one spirit with Jesus. Our sin will never be more powerful than being one with the Lord. His sacrifice is more powerful than all the sins a person can commit. Being one spirit with the Lord, which is salvation, means that eternal life with Him is guaranteed. We'll discuss more about free will later.

When we are born again, He also said that He will never leave us nor relax His hold on us under any circumstance.

Let your character [your moral essence, your inner nature] be free from the love of money [shun greed—be financially ethical], being content with what you have; for He has said, "I will never [under any circumstances] desert you [nor give you up nor leave you without support, nor will I in any degree leave you helpless], nor will I forsake or let you down or relax My hold on you [assuredly not]!" So we take comfort and are encouraged and confidently say,

"The Lord is my Helper [in time of need], I will not be afraid. What will man do to me?" (Heb. 13:5–6, AMP)

11

This confirms the words Jesus had already spoken in John 3:16 and John 10:27–29 (NKJV):

> My sheep hear My voice, and I know them, and they follow Me. And I give them eternal life, and they shall never perish; neither shall anyone snatch them out of My hand. My Father, who has given them to Me, is greater than all; and no one is able to snatch *them out* of My Father's hand.

These verses state that no human being's free will and no demonic being can snatch us out of our Father's hand. Why? Because we are the righteousness of God in Christ Jesus. This perfect location of having our being in Christ Jesus is eternal, not to mention Father God being greater than all.

> He made Christ who knew no sin to [judicially] be sin on our behalf, so that in Him we would become the righteousness of God [that is, we would be made acceptable to Him and placed in a right relationship with Him by His gracious lovingkindness]. (Cor. 5:21, AMP)

Again, this place in Christ Jesus is a place that is untouchable, unmovable, and impervious to any outside influence, no matter our sinful DNA after salvation. The sinful influence from Adam's DNA will be part of our lives as long as we walk in these human bodies, *no matter how sinless we think we are or no matter how sinful we really are.*

Jesus cannot fail. His blood cannot fail. The new covenant (whether we like it or not, whether we received it in its fullness or not) cannot fail! We are cleansed from all unrighteousness because we are the righteousness of God in Christ Jesus. It's not because of any of our works of righteousness, which we may think we perform after salvation. We are righteous because of one act of obedience that Jesus did for us at the cross.

> The Son radiates God's own glory and expresses the very character of God, and he sustains everything by the mighty power of his command. When he had cleansed us from our sins, he sat down in the place of honor at the right hand of the majestic God in heaven. (Heb. 1:3, NLT)

> Even before he made the world, God loved us and chose us in Christ to be holy and without fault in his eyes. God decided in advance to adopt us into his own family by bringing us to himself through Jesus Christ. This is what he wanted to do, and it gave him great pleasure. So we praise God for the glorious grace he has poured out on us who belong to his dear Son. He is so rich in kindness and grace that he purchased our freedom with the blood of his Son and forgave our sins. (Eph. 1:4–7, NLT)

Father God has given us the choice of believing in Jesus or not. It's not a question of whether those who choose to believe in Jesus will be with Him for eternity. Our belief at salvation placed our spirit man with Jesus, seated with Him in heavenly places for eternity.

A side note

The remaining question is whether a person will complete the purpose in the life God gave them or not. The case in point is my life. As I look back at my life, sadly there is no question. I was called by God to preach, as my dad was. I chose to walk a path of self-indulgence instead. It is only by His marvelous grace that I am here now writing this document because I should have died several times during those seasons. By the grace of my God, my pulpit (so to speak) is the marketplace. As my Lord has taught me, no matter where my wife and I go, this truth prevails:

> I will give him the key to the house of David—
> the highest position in the royal court. When he
> opens doors, no one will be able to close them;
> when he closes doors, no one will be able to open
> them. (Isa. 22:22, NLT)

When we submit to Holy Spirit and ask Him to open our eyes to see the open doors to where He is working, divine appointments will be as natural as any conversation we can ever have because it's the Holy Spirit speaking through us. The Holy Spirit knows exactly what to say. God never stops working. He is constantly looking for His child who will say to Him, "Here I am. Send me" (Isa. 6:8, NLT). When Jesus gave us the command of the Great Commission, sending us to the ends of the earth to preach the Gospel, be mindful that, that journey starts at our next-door neighbors and the person we meet at the gas station or anywhere else.

PART 3

The Sin of Rebellion versus the Love of God

One morning, at the age of fifty, I woke up in my car, which was where I had been living for a time due to a drug addiction. I asked God if I could come home to Him, and His love overwhelmed me. I turned to a Christian radio station, and the first sentence that came out was, "What the devil intended for evil, God is now going to turn to good."

I called my dad and asked if I could come live with him and mom for a while. I told Dad that I needed to come home. He said, "I know you do." You see, my preacher dad and mom (as they told me later) had given up on me. Their eyes and any other human eyes that could have watched my life would have thought the same thing. Whatever sin I wanted to do I did. Debauchery was a life style. Death by self-destruction was just a matter of time. Thankfully, they never stopped praying for me, even though they believed I was beyond hope even for God to change my life. My Abba Father had other plans.

A few years later, while my sixth wife and I were driving home, God gave me a download (so to speak) of where Jesus was throughout my life of sinful rebellion. I came home and typed it, as it was given to me in letter form, as I was led to do:

Dear Jesus,

I just wanted to write a letter to You acknowledging a few things I've seen and know You've done in my life. Most importantly, I now see how much You have loved me. It's not because I've ever earned or deserved your love. Love is just who and what You are.

You knew me in the beginning, and you loved me. You knew me at the moment You put me in my mother's womb, and you loved me. You watched me grow and led me to believe in You, and You loved me.

You watched me walk away from You, and I know that hurt You. *But You still loved me.* You did not stop me nor interfere with my free will. As the prodigal son went, so did I. *And You still loved me.* I went out with an inheritance of righteousness and holiness because You are righteous and holy. Your blood made me that way, and You live in me; and in my sin, You never left me. I went into the world and by my own choice became part of the world. I committed every sin my flesh wanted. I did not object but rather enjoyed it all. *And You still loved me.* But just as You said, there is pleasure in sin for a season. My season with sin came crashing down around me. *And You still loved me.*

I was a wreck of a person destroyed by my sin, with nowhere to go and in desperate need of a way out. And there You were waiting for me. *And You still loved me.* You received me back into the flock. The Good Shepherd left the ninety-nine sheep for the one. I had known that scripture, and now that scripture knew me. I was the one You left the ninety-nine for. *You brought me back to You, and You still loved me.*

My Good Shepherd then carried His lamb on His shoulders to recreate the bond between Shepherd and sheep, forming a bond of trust and intimacy stronger than before to keep that little lamb from straying. Thank You, Lord, for carrying me. For You are my God. You didn't have to prove Your faithfulness to me, but You did. *You never stopped loving me.* You said, "I will never leave you nor forsake you." Lord Jesus, I believe You. You proved it. If there was anyone You should have stopped loving and left behind, it is me.

I love You, Jesus, all the more. I am Your child forever because *You still love me.*

Rick

This is when I discovered God's definition of being a child of God. His love for His children does not change because of sin, even if it consumes a major part of a child of God's life, as was the case with me. He is still Abba Father (Daddy God). The sin of wasted years was part of my punishment. All sins have consequences in the flesh. Some results of those years were lives I destroyed, spending every dime I made plus the results of drug and alcohol abuse. Thankfully, from God's standpoint, He poured all His wrath into the body of Jesus on the cross to take care of every sin every believer commits. From Father God's standpoint, Jesus is the perfect and only sacrifice (atonement) for sin required. If this was not so, there is no way the Word of God could state, "I will remember their sins no more." There is no other way we could be spotless before Him without a single fault. There is no other way we could come boldly to our Abba Father's throne of grace and mercy. There is no other reason it is written that mercy triumphs over judgement. There is no other way that the Holy Spirit could live in a believer without ever having to

17

leave that believer after every sin. No matter what, the Holy Spirit will never leave us nor forsake us *ever*!

There is no other way I could still be a child of God.

> I am writing to you who are God's children because your sins have been forgiven through Jesus. (1 John 2:12, NLT)

> Yet now he has reconciled you to himself through the death of Christ in his physical body. As a result, he has brought you into his own presence, and you are holy and blameless as you stand before him without a single fault. (Col. 1:22, NLT)

> Instead, be kind to each other, tenderhearted, forgiving one another, just as God through Christ has forgiven you. (Eph. 4:32, NLT)

Please notice that without exception, none of the scriptures above have any asterisks, denoting any exceptions. *There are no conditions in the new covenant once a person believes in Jesus. Without question, Jesus is God. His sacrifice is perfect. His cleansing blood is perfect. What more than perfection from the I Am that I Am can we possibly think we need for forgivingness of sin? Is it possible for a born again believer to commit a sin that God the Father through Jesus Christ didn't think of to forgive? Unlikely.*

God made grace so simple, but man makes it hard. We tend to look at the new covenant from the standpoint of the Ten Commandments and the Law of Moses instead of the standpoint that salvation is all about Jesus and what He did on the cross for everyone who will believe in Him. Even if a child of God walks away from Him, He will never walk away from one of His children, especially in the midst of that child's sin. My testimony bears witness to this truth. Seriously, is there anything a mere created human being can do that God Almighty, creator of everything, did not do for His creation on the cross? Is it possible that He left anything to chance?

FATHER GOD, AFTER BELIEVING IN JESUS AS SAVIOR, CAN ONE LOSE THEIR SALVATION?

I don't think so. Jesus is still perfect in all His ways; so is His work on the cross.

Let's try and conceive in our human minds what Jesus went through to pay for our sins. Jesus being God is omnipresent. He knows everything all the time and is everywhere all the time (short version of His godship). Here is a case in point:

> And at once some of the scribes said within themselves, "This Man blasphemes!"
> But Jesus, knowing their thoughts, said, "Why do you think evil in your hearts? For which is easier, to say, 'Your sins are forgiven you,' or to say, 'Arise and walk'?" (Matt. 9:3–5, NKJV)

Jesus listens and knows every thought, complaint, ache, pain, and sin of every person not only on the planet at present but every person until His next return. Jesus created time, and while in time, now He stands outside what He created as well—that being time.

Jump ahead in time to when Jesus was on the Mount of Olives praying. Keep in mind that Jesus's memory and knowledge has not changed but was intensified due to the fact that He knows what was coming. God was going to pour all His wrath for the payment for all sin into Jesus's body and redeem all of mankind back to Abba Father, who chose to believe in Jesus as the Son of God.

> Then, accompanied by the disciples, Jesus left the upstairs room and went as usual to the Mount of Olives. There he told them, "Pray that you will not give in to temptation."
> He walked away, about a stone's throw, and knelt down and prayed, "Father, if you are willing, please take this cup of suffering away from me. Yet I want your will to be done, not mine." Then an angel from heaven appeared and strengthened him. He prayed more fervently, and he was in such agony of spirit that his sweat fell

to the ground like great drops of blood. (Luke 22:39–44, NLT)

[Pilate said,] "So I will have him flogged, and then I will release him."

Then a mighty roar rose from the crowd, and with one voice they shouted, "Kill him, and release Barabbas to us!" (Barabbas was in prison for taking part in an insurrection in Jerusalem against the government, and for murder.) Pilate argued with them, because he wanted to release Jesus. But they kept shouting, "Crucify him! Crucify him!"

For the third time he demanded, "Why? What crime has he committed? I have found no reason to sentence him to death. So I will have him flogged, and then I will release him."

But the mob shouted louder and louder, demanding that Jesus be crucified, and their voices prevailed. So Pilate sentenced Jesus to die as they demanded. As they had requested, he released Barabbas, the man in prison for insurrection and murder. But he turned Jesus over to them to do as they wished. (Luke 23:16–25, NLT)

By this time it was about noon, and darkness fell across the whole land until three o'clock. The light from the sun was gone. And suddenly, the curtain in the sanctuary of the Temple was torn down the middle. Then Jesus shouted, "Father, I entrust my spirit into your hands!" And with those words he breathed his last.

When the Roman officer overseeing the execution saw what had happened, he worshiped God and said, "Surely this man was innocent." And when all the crowd that came to see the crucifixion saw what had happened, they went home in deep sorrow. But Jesus' friends, including the women who had followed him from Galilee, stood at a distance watching. (Luke 23:44–49, NLT)

Remember Isaiah's prophecy approximately seven hundred years prior to the actual events of our Lords suffering for His creation?

Who has believed our message?
To whom has the Lord revealed his powerful arm?
My servant grew up in the Lord's presence like a tender
    green shoot,
like a root in dry ground.
There was nothing beautiful or majestic about his
    appearance,
nothing to attract us to him.
He was despised and rejected—
a man of sorrows, acquainted with deepest grief.
We turned our backs on him and looked the other way.
He was despised, and we did not care.
Yet it was our weaknesses he carried;
it was our sorrows that weighed him down.
And we thought his troubles were a punishment from God,
a punishment for his own sins!
But he was pierced for our rebellion,
crushed for our sins.
He was beaten so we could be whole.
He was whipped so we could be healed.
All of us, like sheep, have strayed away.
We have left God's paths to follow our own.
Yet the Lord laid on him
the sins of us all.
He was oppressed and treated harshly,
yet he never said a word.
He was led like a lamb to the slaughter.
And as a sheep is silent before the shearers,

he did not open his mouth.
Unjustly condemned,
he was led away.
No one cared that he died without descendants,
that his life was cut short in midstream.
But he was struck down
for the rebellion of my people.
He had done no wrong
and had never deceived anyone.
But he was buried like a criminal;
he was put in a rich man's grave.
But it was the Lord's good plan to crush him
and cause him grief.
Yet when his life is made an offering for sin,
he will have many descendants.
He will enjoy a long life,
and the Lord's good plan will prosper in his hands.
When he sees all that is accomplished by his anguish,
he will be satisfied.
And because of his experience,
my righteous servant will make it possible
for many to be counted righteous,
for he will bear all their sins.
I will give him the honors of a victorious soldier,
because he exposed himself to death.
He was counted among the rebels.
He bore the sins of many and interceded for rebels. (Isa.
    53:1–12, NLT)

Seeing the complete picture of the blood covenant of Jesus and the new covenant leaves no possibility for a believer in Jesus Christ to lose their salvation or have an unforgiven sin.

PART 4

After Jesus Did It All on the Cross, What About the Sins We Still Commit?

To add clarity to what has already been written about God's memory being perfect, He never forgets anything unless He promises otherwise.

> "But this is the new covenant I will make with the people of Israel after those days," says the Lord. "I will put my instructions deep within them, and I will write them on their hearts. I will be their God, and they will be my people. And they will not need to teach their neighbors, nor will they need to teach their relatives, saying, 'You should know the Lord.' For everyone, from the least to the greatest, will know me already," says the Lord. "And I will forgive their wickedness, and I will never again remember their sins." (Jer. 31:33–34, NLT)

> And I will forgive their wickedness, and I will never again remember their sins."

> When God speaks of a "new" covenant, it means he has made the first one obsolete. It is

now out of date and will soon disappear. (Heb. 8:12–13, NLT)

Every priest stands [at his altar of service] ministering daily, offering the same sacrifices over and over, which are never able to strip away sins [that envelop and cover us]; whereas Christ, having offered the one sacrifice [the all-sufficient sacrifice of Himself] for sins for all time, sat down [signifying the completion of atonement for sin] at the right hand of God [the position of honor], waiting from that time onward until his enemies are made a footstool for His feet. For by the one offering He has perfected forever and completely cleansed those who are being sanctified [bringing each believer to spiritual completion and maturity]. And the Holy Spirit also adds His testimony to us [in confirmation of this]; for after having said,

"This is the covenant that I will make with them
After those days, says the Lord:
I will imprint My laws upon their heart,
And on their mind I will inscribe them [producing an inward change],"

He then says,

"And their sins and their lawless acts I will remember no more [no longer holding their sins against them]."

Now where there is [absolute] forgiveness *and* complete cancellation of the penalty of these things, there is no longer any offering [to be made to atone] for sin. (Heb. 10:11–18, AMP)

FATHER GOD, AFTER BELIEVING IN JESUS AS SAVIOR, CAN ONE LOSE THEIR SALVATION?

God made this covenant divinely perfect so no one like Adam and Eve or you and me could mess it up.

How can one lose their salvation when God won't remember our sins and confirms this by stating that there is no judgement against anyone who believes in Jesus?

I implore you not to skip over these verses. *Not* fully considering the context, depth and magnitude of these few scriptures has allowed us to believe we can lose our salvation. *If we fully understood what these few verses stated, there would be no need for this document.*

> "For this is how God loved the world: He gave his one and only Son, so that everyone who believes in him will not perish but have eternal life. God sent his Son into the world not to judge the world, but to save the world through him.
>
> "There is no judgment against anyone who believes in him. But anyone who does not believe in him has already been judged for not believing in God's one and only Son. (John 3:16–18, NLT)

Jesus also said;

> I have come as a light to shine in this dark world, so that all who put their trust in me will no longer remain in the dark. I will not judge those who hear me but don't obey me, for I have come to save the world and not to judge it. But all who reject me and my message will be judged on the day of judgment by the truth I have spoken. I don't speak on my own authority. The Father who sent me has commanded me what to say and how to say it. And I know his commands lead to eternal life; so I say whatever the Father tells me to say." John 12:46-50 NLT

PART 5

God's Family

> He came to His own, and His own did not
> receive Him. But as many as received Him, to
> them He gave the right to become children of
> God, to those who believe in His name: who
> were born, not of blood, nor of the will of the
> flesh, nor of the will of man, but of God. (John
> 1:11–13, NKJV)

When one is born of God (or born again), they are a child of God
forever. When a person becomes rebellious or backslides, that doesn't
change God's unchangeable mind about their eternity. At times, we
need to step back and remember that God has been dealing with rebellious children since the original rebellious children, Adam and Eve.

> Then he said, "There was once a man who had
> two sons. The younger said to his father, 'Father,
> I want right now what's coming to me.'
> "So the father divided the property between
> them. It wasn't long before the younger son
> packed his bags and left for a distant country.
> There, undisciplined and dissipated, he wasted
> everything he had. After he had gone through all
> his money, there was a bad famine all through

that country and he began to hurt. He signed on with a citizen there who assigned him to his fields to slop the pigs. He was so hungry he would have eaten the corncobs in the pig slop, but no one would give him any.

"That brought him to his senses. He said, 'All those farmhands working for my father sit down to three meals a day, and here I am starving to death. I'm going back to my father. I'll say to him, Father, I've sinned against God, I've sinned before you; I don't deserve to be called your son. Take me on as a hired hand.' He got right up and went home to his father.

"When he was still a long way off, his father saw him. His heart pounding, he ran out, embraced him, and kissed him. The son started his speech: 'Father, I've sinned against God, I've sinned before you; I don't deserve to be called your son ever again.'

"But the father wasn't listening. He was calling to the servants, 'Quick. Bring a clean set of clothes and dress him. Put the family ring on his finger and sandals on his feet. Then get a grain-fed heifer and roast it. We're going to feast! We're going to have a wonderful time! My son is here— given up for dead and now alive! Given up for lost and now found!' And they began to have a wonderful time. (Luke 15:11–24, MSG)

When I was born again at the age of five, I became a child of God. I was a child of God by a rebirth of Spirit and water. I willingly left the path God wanted for me and my life for the lust of the flesh, just like the prodigal son. I also hit a rock bottom, and instinctively, I needed to go home to my Heavenly Father out of utter desperation.

The prodigal son was given up for dead and given up for lost, but *he was never not a son of God*. The father in this story is an earthly father representing our Heavenly Farther who never leaves us nor forsakes us. Rather, God gives us full reign of our free will in the hopes of a greater relationship with Him here on earth. But for those who abuse the grace and love of God to the ends of their lives and don't fulfill the plan of God for their lives, they are still children of God because God's covenant of grace is perfect, and our sins are cleansed. Once we are born again, there is no way to be spiritually unborn. Once we become a child of God, there is no way not to be a child of God. In this case, we seem to lack full understanding of the limitations of free will. After we believe in Jesus, our free will has limitations. More on free will shall come shortly.

> For He whom God has sent speaks the words of God, for God does not give the Spirit by measure. The Father loves the Son and has given all things into His hand. He who believes in the Son has everlasting life; and he who does not believe the Son shall not see life, but the wrath of God abides on him." (John 3:34–36, NKJV)

> "I tell you the truth, those who listen to my message and believe in God who sent me have eternal life. They will never be condemned for their sins, but they have already passed from death into life. (John 5:24, NLT)

God is still God, no matter if a believer has an intimate, loving relationship with Him or rages at Him like a three-year-old child. The part of a person that loves God or rages at God is in the mind, will, and emotion areas of our beings. Remember, our spirit man is seated in heavenly places with Christ Jesus, impervious to the emotional drama that comes with being a human being. We have passed from death onto a life that is untouchable and unchangeable by any human influence or action.

PART 6

Back to the Basics or what I Relate to Better, "Keeping It Simple…"

Is it possible to be overfamiliar with a scripture? *Yes*!

The case in point is where we began with this document. All that is really needed to be quoted as an answer to the question, "Can we lose our salvation?" is John 3:16. We know it so well that we never acknowledged it to the point of understanding three words: *will not perish*.

> For this is how God loved the world: He gave his one and only Son, so that everyone who believes in him will not perish but have eternal life. (John 3:16, NLT)

When Jesus spoke these words, He did not include any conditions, except for believing in Him! When we see something that looks too good to be true, it usually is. The factual reality is that the God-man Jesus walked in the flesh of humanity. He knows and understands every weakness. Father God and Jesus's design of the new covenant took every frailty of the human condition in mind and made a foolproof new covenant. In doing so, Jesus is saying that there is absolutely no way a person who believes in Him can lose his or her salvation. Jesus made it impossible for our sinful weaknesses or lack of understanding to cause us to lose our salvation. Our position now is that we are one with Jesus. Other versions say in Christ Jesus,

> God has united you with Christ Jesus. For our benefit God made him to be wisdom itself. Christ made us right with God; he made us pure and holy, and he freed us from sin. (1 Cor. 1:30, NLT)

Once we are in or one with Christ Jesus, we can't lose our salvation, no matter our faithless disobedience, due to the simple fact that Jesus is the one and only faithful one; and He cannot lie.

> If we are unfaithful, he remains faithful, for he cannot deny who he is. (2 Tim. 2:13, NLT)

> This letter is from Paul, a slave of God and an apostle of Jesus Christ. I have been sent to proclaim faith to those God has chosen and to teach them to know the truth that shows them how to live godly lives. This truth gives them confidence that they have eternal life, which God—who does not lie—promised them before the world began. (Titus 1:1–2, NLT)

As stated before, over the many years of my life, there was no out of bounds for my actions. I have three DUIs, there weren't many drugs I didn't like and, as you already know, I have been married six times.

This marriage is the only marriage that was founded in Jesus. Jesus will always be first from both our standpoints.

This document or the grace of God does not provide a license to sin! The actions of sin, as defined by the Law, is still a detriment for humanity. God still hates sin. We still hate sin. Sin is still the opposite of holiness and righteousness. Instead, the new covenant of grace provides the privilege to commune with the Father and go boldly before His throne any time, especially when we sin, so our paths can be realigned with that of our Father's. Abba Father has made it possible to be in His presence in a personal nonstop relationship. He had to completely deal with our sin for this to happen, for our God is a holy God. We have had access to Abba Father since the curtain was torn in two at the death of Jesus.

PART 7

Free Will

As stated earlier, once we are seated in heavenly places with Christ Jesus, we are beyond the influence of our free will regarding our eternal destination. We are with Jesus for all eternity.

Equally so, if a person dies without believing in Jesus, their free will also no longer has any influence regarding their eternal destination. They are lost for all eternity. They are also no longer in the earthly realm.

Therefore, regarding salvation, our free will to change our eternal destination ends when our spirit man leaves the earthly realm.

Here's what we need to remember:

> No, don't say that. Who are you, a mere human being, to argue with God? Should the thing that was created say to the one who created it, "Why have you made me like this?" When a potter makes jars out of clay, doesn't he have a right to use the same lump of clay to make one jar for decoration and another to throw garbage into it? (Rom. 9:20–21, NLT)

Every person makes things in their life. Whatever is made belongs to that person. So, it is with mankind. Even though we

want to forget we must not forget we are made by God for His good
pleasure.

Literally, look at humanity from God's perspective; and at the
same time, take a look at His person:

> In front of the throne was a shiny sea of glass,
> sparkling like crystal.
>
> In the center and around the throne were
> four living beings, each covered with eyes, front
> and back. The first of these living beings was like
> a lion; the second was like an ox; the third had a
> human face; and the fourth was like an eagle in
> flight. Each of these living beings had six wings,
> and their wings were covered all over with eyes,
> inside and out. Day after day and night after
> night they keep on saying,
>
> "Holy, holy, holy is the Lord God, the Almighty—
> the one who always was, who is, and who is still
> to come."
>
> Whenever the living beings give glory and honor
> and thanks to the one sitting on the throne (the
> one who lives forever and ever), the twenty-four
> elders fall down and worship the one sitting on the
> throne (the one who lives forever and ever). And
> they lay their crowns before the throne and say,
>
> "You are worthy, O Lord our God, to receive
> glory and honor and power.
>
> For you created all things, and they exist
> because you created what you pleased." (Rev.
> 4:6–11, NLT)

In the beginning the Word already existed.

> The Word was with God, and the Word was God.
> He existed in the beginning with God.
> God created everything through him, and nothing was created except through him.
> The Word gave life to everything that was created, and his life brought light to everyone. (John 1:1–4, NLT)

Clearly, Jesus is Jesus, and we are not. To think Father God would place our sin above the sacrifice of His Son Jesus (described above) clearly gives sin a place of power and authority above the power and authority of Jesus and His cleansing blood. This would have to be the case for someone to lose their salvation, and clearly it is not.

> After Jesus said this, he looked toward heaven and prayed: "Father, the hour has come. Glorify your Son, that your Son may glorify you. For you granted him authority over all people that he might give eternal life to all those you have given him. (John 17:1–2, NLT)

> But our High Priest offered himself to God as a single sacrifice for sins, good for all time. Then he sat down in the place of honor at God's right hand. There he waits until his enemies are humbled and made a footstool under his feet. (Heb. 10:12–13, NLT)

Clearly, this is not the case. Sin does not have power and authority over the one sacrifice for sin for all time that Jesus provided for believers.

PART 8

Frequently Asked Questions or in the Case of, "Can One Lose One's Salvation?" the What Abouts...

Scenario 1—What about one's sin after salvation, as quoted by the apostle Paul?

> For the wages of sin is death, but the free gift of God is eternal life through Christ Jesus our Lord. (Rom. 6:23, NLT)

Is Paul expecting us not to sin? And if we do, are we not qualified for God's free gift of eternal life?

The apostle Paul seems to send mixed messages at times. In the scriptures presented prior in this document, he states that God, through Christ, has forgiven us; and we have eternal life. He states in Ephesians 5 below that we are God's children:

> Imitate God, therefore, in everything you do, because you are his dear children. (Eph. 5:1, NLT)

Then a scripture later, Paul seems to retreat to his days as a Pharisee and the Law of Moses and condemnation, or so I thought at one time, when he states,

Let there be no sexual immorality, impurity, or greed among you. Such sins have no place among God's people. Obscene stories, foolish talk, and coarse jokes—these <u>are not for you</u>. Instead, let there be thankfulness to God. You can be sure that no immoral, impure, or greedy person will inherit the Kingdom of Christ and of God. For a greedy person is an idolater, worshiping the things of this world.

Don't be fooled by those who try to excuse these sins, for the anger of God will fall on all who disobey him. Don't participate in the things these people do. (Eph. 5:3–7, NLT)

In verses 4 and 7, the terms "are not for you and these people" show us that this group of people are not saved. In Ephesians 4:32, a chapter earlier, God's people have their sins already forgiven through Christ. The above sins do have consequence's in the flesh but no punishment from God. God has chosen not to remember our sins. Again, how can He punish us for what He doesn't remember? And what the blood of Jesus has cleansed us from?

How then did Jesus himself define sin under the new covenant?

But now I am going away to the one who sent me, and not one of you is asking where I am going. Instead, you grieve because of what I've told you. But in fact, it is best for you that I go away, because if I don't, the Advocate won't come. If I do go away, then I will send him to you. And when he comes, he will convict the world of its sin, and of God's righteousness, and of the coming judgment. The world's sin is that it refuses to believe in me. Righteousness is available because I go to the Father, and you will see me no more. Judgment will come because the ruler of this world has already been judged. (John 16:5–11, NLT)

Please note that in verses 8 and 9, sin is singular, not plural. There is one judgeable sin from Jesus', standpoint—not believing in Him.

This confirms what Jesus said earlier in John 3: 16–18 (NLT). Also, in the apostle Paul's first sermon of preaching the Good News, the Gospel of grace, in Acts 13:13–43 (NLT), Paul defines what the result of believing in Jesus does:

> Brothers, listen! We are here to proclaim that through this man Jesus there is forgiveness for your sins. Everyone who believes in him is made right in God's sight—something the law of Moses could never do. (Acts 13:38–39, NLT)

Father God poured out all the sins of the world and all His wrath for sin into the body of Jesus at the cross. There are no more consequences for sin for believers from God at all. Do consequences remain in the flesh for sin? Absolutely. Again, God hates sin. We hate sin, and that will never change.

> But now God has shown us a way to be made right with him without keeping the requirements of the law, as was promised in the writings of Moses and the prophets long ago. We are made right with God by placing our faith in Jesus Christ. And this is true for everyone who believes, no matter who we are. (Rom. 3:21–22, NLT)

That being said, the apostle Paul had to deal with the liberties of the new covenant, which some wanted to exploit:

> You say, "I am allowed to do anything"—but not everything is good for you. And even though "I am allowed to do anything," I must not become a slave to anything. You say, "Food was made for the stomach, and the stomach for food." (This is

true, though someday God will do away with both of them.) But you can't say that our bodies were made for sexual immorality. They were made for the Lord, and the Lord cares about our bodies. And God will raise us from the dead by his power, just as he raised our Lord from the dead.

Don't you realize that your bodies are actually parts of Christ? Should a man take his body, which is part of Christ, and join it to a prostitute? Never! And don't you realize that if a man joins himself to a prostitute, he becomes one body with her? For the Scriptures say, "The two are united into one." But the person who is joined to the Lord is one spirit with him

Run from sexual sin! No other sin so clearly affects the body as this one does. For sexual immorality is a sin against your own body. Don't you realize that your body is the temple of the Holy Spirit, who lives in you and was given to you by God? You do not belong to yourself, for God bought you with a high price. So you must honor God with your body. (1 Cor. 6:12–20, NLT)

Is there a consequence for sin (as sin is defined in the Law of Moses) for believers? Again, most definitely yes. The consequences come as a natural reaction in the flesh. Sin also causes a distraction of focus regarding our faith. Any sin, as defined by the Law of Moses, was purposed to show man what not to do. Under the Law, God required a sin offering for forgiveness. Before the Law, man committed the same sins; but since there was no Law to break, there was no punishment from God for those same sins. In Hebrews 10 (NLT), Jesus made the Law of Moses obsolete, but the consequences for those sins remain in the flesh, just like in Abraham's time.

Then he said, "Look, I have come to do your will."
He cancels the first covenant in order to put the

second into effect. For God's will was for us to
be made holy by the sacrifice of the body of Jesus
Christ, once for all time. (Heb.10:9–10, NLT)

Also,

> When you were dead in your sins and in the
> uncircumcision your flesh (worldliness, manner
> of life), God made you alive together with Christ,
> having [freely] forgiven us all our sins, having
> canceled out the certificate of debt consisting of
> legal demands [which were in force] against us
> and which were hostile to us. And this certificate
> He has set aside and completely removed by nail-
> ing it to the cross. (Col. 2:13–14, AMP)

The certificate of debt, with all its legal demands that is now
canceled, is the Law of Moses. Once again, there is no Law to break,
just as in the time of Abraham. That is why in Hebrews 9:28 (NLT)
it is written,

> So also Christ was offered once for all time as a sac-
> rifice to take away the sins of many people. He will
> come again, not to deal with our sins, but to bring
> salvation to all who are eagerly waiting for him.

Jesus will not come again to deal with our sins because all believers' sins were dealt with on the cross (Hebrews 10:11–12).

Scenario 2—What about renouncing Jesus and His salvation?

> When people work, their wages are not a gift,
> but something they have earned. But people are
> counted as righteous, not because of their work,
> but because of their faith in God who forgives sin-
> ners. David also spoke of this when he described

the happiness of those who are declared righteous without working for it:

> "Oh, what joy for those whose disobedience is forgiven, whose sins are put out of sight.
> Yes, what joy for those whose record the Lord has cleared of sin." (Rom. 4:4–8, NLT)

To give back the gift of righteousness and renounce Jesus and one's salvation is childish emotional rebellion. When I experienced this, it was out of rage, anger, and hatred, which are sins under the Law. Again, God does not remember ours sins any longer.

I speak for myself when I state this truth: the new covenant is foolproof.

Scenario 3—What about 1 John 1:9? Can one lose one's salvation if one doesn't confess one's sins for forgiveness?

> But if we confess our sins to him, he is faithful and just to forgive us our sins and to cleanse us from all wickedness. (1 John 1:9, NLT)

The root of confession for forgiveness of sin is found in Leviticus 5:4–6 (NKJV):

> Or if a person swears, speaking thoughtlessly with *his* lips to do evil or to do good, whatever it is that a man may pronounce by an oath, and he is unaware of it—when he realizes *it*, then he shall be guilty in any of these matters.
> And it shall be, when he is guilty in any of these matters, that he shall confess that he has sinned in that thing; and he shall bring his trespass offering to the Lord for his sin which he has committed, a female from the flock, a lamb or a

kid of the goats as a sin offering. So, the priest
shall make atonement for him concerning his sin.

Since the root of confession for forgiveness of sin is part of the
Law of Moses—and the Law of Moses Jesus made obsolete on His
cross—by default, confession of sins for forgiveness of sins *after salvation is obsolete.* Jesus is now and forever the all-sufficient sacrifice for
our sins (1 Corinthians 1:2, 1 Corinthians 6:11, Romans 10:3, Acts
10:42–44, and many others).

To further add clarity to this understanding, we'll look at
Hebrews 10 again:

> Every priest stands [at his altar of service] ministering daily, offering the same sacrifices over and
> over, which are never able to strip away sins [that
> envelop and cover us]; whereas Christ, having
> offered the one sacrifice [the all-sufficient sacrifice of Himself] for sins for all time, sat down
> [signifying the completion of atonement for sin]
> at the right hand of God [the position of honor],
> waiting from that time onward until his enemies
> are made a footstool for His feet. For by the one
> offering He has perfected forever and completely
> cleansed those who are being sanctified [bringing
> each believer to spiritual completion and maturity]. And the Holy Spirit also adds His testimony to us [in confirmation of this]; for after
> having said,
>
> "This is the covenant that I will make with them
> After those days, says the Lord:
> I will imprint My laws upon their heart,
> And on their mind I will inscribe them [producing an inward change],"

He then says,

"And their sins and their lawless acts
     I will remember no more [no longer hold-
ing their sins against them]"

Now where there is [absolute] forgiveness and complete cancellation of the penalty of these things, there is no longer any offering [to be made to atone] for sin. (Heb. 10:11–18, AMP)

Confessing one's sins after salvation for forgiveness of sin is in fact an atonement for sin. Jesus's atonement is complete for all sins, yet some believe we still must confess sins to be forgiven of sins. That means one's confession is only good until their next sin, which is much like—if not just like—verse 11 and nothing like verse 12. Either Jesus is enough, or He isn't. Either Jesus's sacrifice is enough, or it's not. Either Jesus made the Law obsolete and ushered in a new covenant for believers, or He didn't. Perhaps the hardest point to understand is that the new covenant only has one thing in common with the old covenant—that is Jesus wrote them both. Other than that, they are as opposite as they can be. The Law was a covenant of requirement and demand; the new covenant of grace is a covenant of supply. In the old covenant, man supplied an animal for his own sin sacrifice. In the new covenant, God gave His one and only Son as a sacrifice for all sins.

If the first covenant had been faultless, there would have been no need for a second covenant to replace it. But when God found fault with the people, he said:

"The day is coming, says the Lord, when I will make a new covenant with the people of Israel and Judah.

> This covenant will not be like the one I made with their ancestors when I took them by the hand and led them out of the land of Egypt.
> They did not remain faithful to my covenant, so I turned my back on them, says the Lord.
> But this is the new covenant I will make with the people of Israel on that day, says the Lord:
> I will put my laws in their minds, and I will write them on their hearts.
> I will be their God, and they will be my people.
> And they will not need to teach their neighbors, nor will they need to teach their relatives, saying, 'You should know the Lord.'
> For everyone, from the least to the greatest, will know me already.
> And I will forgive their wickedness, and I will never again remember their sins."
>
> When God speaks of a "new" covenant, it means he has made the first one obsolete. It is now out of date and will soon disappear. (Heb. 8:7–13, NLT)

The Bible makes it very clear that the sacrifice of Jesus is all-sufficient for sin, and through His work on the cross there is complete forgiveness of sins. *When the Bible states there is no longer any offering to be made for or to atone for sin, our future sins are forgiven as well,* affirming that confession for sins after salvation is for relationship and out of love but not required for forgiveness of sins. Jesus wants our attention to be given to Him out of and for love rather than fear of a righteous punishment. He wants His bride to be in love with Him, for our wedding day approaches.

> Let us rejoice and shout for joy! Let us give Him glory and honor, for the marriage of the Lamb

has come [at last] and His bride (the redeemed) has prepared herself. (Rev. 19:7, AMP)

Remember,

> So we praise God for the glorious grace he has poured out on us who belong to his dear Son. He is so rich in kindness and grace that he purchased our freedom with the blood of his Son and forgave our sins. (Eph. 1:6–7, NLT)

Those who belong to His dear Son are those who are born again. He forgave all sins at that point, including all future sins.

All that being said, John, therefore, was speaking this testimony in 1 John:1–10 to unbelievers in hopes that they would accept Jesus as Lord in context. As historically recorded, these were gnostic Jews who do not believe in Jesus as the Messiah. In the opening scriptures of 1 John 1, there was no greeting of affection as in 1 John 2. When speaking to God's children (born-again Jews), John used terms of affection in those greetings, such as "my dear children" or "my beloved." This is confirmed by his statement to his new audience,

> My dear children, I am writing this to you so that you will not sin. But if anyone does sin, we have an advocate who pleads our case before the Father. He is Jesus Christ, the one who is truly righteous. He himself is the sacrifice that atones for our sins—and not only our sins but the sins of all the world. (1 John 2:1–2, NLT)

If confession of sins for forgiveness of sins was John's intent, verse 2 would have included, "as long as you confess your sins to Jesus" because John was speaking to believers at this time. Clearly this is not the case.

From 1 John 1:1 to 1 John 2:1, there is a distinct difference in audiences.

Not only that, but John puts it in writing that He Himself (Jesus) is the sacrifice that atones for sin, not confession after salvation. If confession was needed in addition to Jesus's sacrifice, John or some other apostle would have said so. No such commandment exists in the new covenant.

Confession under the new covenant is out of relationship and intimacy because we have already been forgiven (Ephesians 4:32, NLT).

We see now that the Word of God has made it overwhelmingly clear at salvation that all past, present, and future sins are cleansed; and there will be no further judgement against us from God.

> Since we have now been justified by his blood, how much more shall we be saved from God's wrath through him! For if, while we were God's enemies, we were reconciled to him through the death of his Son, how much more, having been reconciled, shall we be saved through his life! (Rom. 5:9–10, NLT)

We born-again believers stand before God cleansed and without fault. God designed this covenant in this manner because of the sinful DNA that remained from Adam and Eve.

When Noah got off the ark, he built an altar. Remember when God declared Noah the only righteous man on earth? Note God's first comment about the condition of humanity when Noah got off the ark. God resonates this condition throughout history.

> Then Noah built an altar to the Lord, and there he sacrificed as burnt offerings the animals and birds that had been approved for that purpose. And the Lord was pleased with the aroma of the sacrifice and said to himself, "I will never again curse the ground because of the human race, even though everything they think or imagine is bent toward evil from childhood. I will never again destroy all living things. (Gen. 8:20–21, NLT)

But we are all like an unclean thing, And all our righteousness's are like filthy rags; We all fade as a leaf, And our iniquities, like the wind, Have taken us away. (Isa. 64:6, NKJV)

The human heart is the most deceitful of all things, and desperately wicked. Who really knows how bad it is? (Jer. 17:9, NLT)

The apostle Paul really summed up the sinful plight of humanity:

And I know that nothing good lives in me, that is, in my sinful nature. I want to do what is right, but I can't. I want to do what is good, but I don't. I don't want to do what is wrong, but I do it anyway. But if I do what I don't want to do, I am not really the one doing wrong; it is sin living in me that does it. (Rom. 7:1819, NLT)

We, as children of God, believe at times that we can go through a day or days without sinning. Based on the above scriptures that is probably impossible. As a result, complete and total confession would seem unlikely. We believe we can go through a day without sinning because we look at sin through our eyes and the lens of the Ten Commandments *based on our own understanding* rather than the eyes of a perfect and holy God who says,

"My thoughts are nothing like your thoughts," says the Lord.

"And my ways are far beyond anything you could imagine.
For just as the heavens are higher than the earth, so my ways are higher than your ways and my thoughts higher than your thoughts". (Isa. 55:8–9, NLT)

FATHER GOD, AFTER BELIEVING IN JESUS AS SAVIOR, CAN ONE LOSE THEIR SALVATION?

The same mindset that leads us to believe we can go a day without sinning applies to our thoughts about a child of God losing their salvation. Please remember we are *the created, not the Creator*. We *are not* to be the Judge; we are the judged. According to the Word of God, His judgment for eternity is determined by whether one believes in Father God's one and only Son Jesus or not. Our *tendency* is to make His judgment based on our understanding of sin. His judgement of our sin is not based on our sin, as defined by the Law of Moses, but rather if we believe in Jesus or not. Assuming the judgment seat of Jesus, the Just Judge, and judging someone who seems to have gone so far in sin that they have lost their salvation and are out of the grasp of Jesus is nothing more than self-righteousness, just like the Pharisees. At this point, aren't we ever so grateful that God has cleansed us of all our sins and remembers them no more? Aren't we grateful that God changed everything for us at the cross of our precious Lord and Savior (Romans 5:1–21)? Under the new covenant, no one goes to hell because of sin. One goes to hell by not believing in Jesus Christ as one's personal Lord and Savior.

In the Gospels when Jesus healed bodies and forgave sins, there is no record of Jesus requiring a confession or an act of repentance. If all we had to do is confess our sins and repent of our sins, what did Jesus die for? Even the thief on the cross by Jesus didn't confess or repent. But after the thief acknowledged who Jesus was, Jesus said, "This day you will be with Me in Paradise" (Luke 23:42–43, NKJV). The thief on the cross was one of the very first born-again human beings on the planet. What a picture of who salvation is for. What a picture of God's love for the humanity He created and the salvation process. What a picture of the perfection of the new covenant.

The verse 1 John 1:9 is directed at nonbelievers as roadmap to their salvation, as laid out in the first chapter of 1 John.

The only thing stated regarding confession for forgiveness of sin is this:

> But what does it say? "The word is near you, in
> your mouth and in your heart" (that is, the word
> of faith which we preach): that if you confess with

your mouth the Lord Jesus and believe in your heart that God has raised Him from the dead, you will be saved. For with the heart one believes unto righteousness, and with the mouth confession is made unto salvation. For the Scripture says, "Whoever believes on Him will not be put to shame." (Rom. 10:8–11, NKJV)

The apostle Paul states this confession unto salvation as a declaration of believing in Jesus versus an itemized list of sins to be forgiven.

Here's what the Just Judge Jesus said that we need to confess:

Therefore whoever confesses Me before men, him I will also confess before My Father who is in heaven. But whoever denies Me before men, him I will also deny before My Father who is in heaven. (Matt. 10:32–33, NKJV)

There is nothing to confess for forgiveness of sins by the One who will judge us.

In the book of James, James states about confession for healing:

Confess your trespasses to one another, and pray for one another, that you may be healed. The effective, fervent prayer of a righteous man avails much. (James 5:16, NKJV)

In context, James's intent is to free oneself of guilt by confessing one's sins to one another. A guilty conscience is a faith deterrent, not allowing divine healing to occur due to an opinion of oneself of unworthiness. In fact, Jesus's sacrifice has made every believer worthy. We receive His righteousness at salvation; He received our sins in His body at the cross. As a result of this divine exchange, Jesus made us worthy so we could have intimacy and access to Abba Father, Jesus Himself, and Holy Spirit.

Do I confess and repent? Yes. Because I love my God, I do this out of intimacy because I know I have already been forgiven.

Under the new covenant, God left nothing to chance. There is no possible way for a born-again believer to be able to receive God's wrath or lose the salvation Jesus paid for with such a high price.

Scenario 4—What about Hebrews 6 (NLT)?

> For it is impossible to bring back to repentance those who were once enlightened—those who have experienced the good things of heaven and shared in the Holy Spirit, who have tasted the goodness of the word of God and the power of the age to come—and who then turn away from God. It is impossible to bring such people back to repentance; by rejecting the Son of God, they themselves are nailing him to the cross once again and holding him up to public shame. (Heb. 6:4–6, NLT)

A state of enlightenment is a mental understanding of Jesus and the power of His name but without personally knowing Him i.e., the sons of Scevia (Acts 19:11–20, NLT). A heart understanding is an intimate progression of knowing and coming to accept Jesus as one's personal Lord and Savior.

Most of my life, I turned away from God, which led me to believe that I lost my salvation and fell from grace. In those seasons, because of these scriptures and scriptures like these that go against the grace of God, I thought I rejected Jesus or He rejected me. In reading these scriptures in Hebrews 6, from the standpoint of having been saved, I was unable to come back to Him. I just didn't understand.

I will use our church experience in hopes of providing an understanding of the above scriptures.

In our worship service, the Holy Spirit's presence is tangible. God inhabits the praises of His people. The Word of God goes forth in the pastor's sermon. This experience fulfills experiencing the good things of heaven and the age to come. There is enlightenment. If at the invitation to receive Jesus as Lord, the answer is no to salvation, enlightenment remains. A person still has the awareness of that experience. Enlightenment is spiritual awareness or head knowledge. Salvation is heart knowledge, fully believing in Jesus, providing a new birth (being born again).

Hebrews 6:4–6 was not written about believers, but unbelievers.

Scenario 5—What about the Final Judgement in Revelation 20?

> And I saw a great white throne and the one sitting on it. The earth and sky fled from his presence, but they found no place to hide. I saw the dead, both great and small, standing before God's throne. And the books were opened, including the Book of Life. And the dead were judged according to what they had done, as recorded in the books. The sea gave up its dead, and death and the grave gave up their dead. And all were judged according to their deeds. Then death and the grave were thrown into the lake of fire. This lake of fire is the second death. And anyone whose name was not found recorded in the Book of Life was thrown into the lake of fire. (Rev. 20:11–15, NLT)

Please note in verse 12 that the word books is plural. From our standpoint, the only book we are recorded in as born-again believers in Jesus is the Book of Life. Also, in verse 12, we will be judged for all our deeds, as recorded in the books. We will not be judged for our sins because they are cleansed and remembered no more.

Our judgement will come at the Bema Seat of Christ. The term Bema Seat stems from the original Olympics where a judge sat on that seat and determined the winners of competitions and the appropriate honors. Jesus bore all our sins at the cross so there would be no judgement for our sins, just rewards at His Bema Seat. To judge believers' sins again would be double jeopardy.

> Since we have now been justified by his blood, how much more shall we be saved from God's wrath through him! For if, while we were God's enemies, we were reconciled to him through the death of his Son, how much more, having been reconciled, shall we be saved through his life! Not only is this so, but we also boast in God through our Lord Jesus Christ, through whom we have now received reconciliation. (Rom. 5:9–11, NIV)

Scenario 6—What about when I knowingly or deliberately sin?

> Dear friends, if we deliberately continue sinning after we have received knowledge of the truth, there is no longer any sacrifice that will cover these sins. There is only the terrible expectation of God's judgment and the raging fire that will consume his enemies. For anyone who refused to obey the law of Moses was put to death without mercy on the testimony of two or three witnesses. Just think how much worse the punishment will be for those who have trampled on the Son of God, and have treated the blood of the covenant, which made us holy, as if it were common and unholy, and have insulted and disdained the Holy Spirit who brings God's mercy to us. (Heb. 10:26–29, NLT)

No one is an enemy of God after believing in Jesus as Lord.
The book of Hebrews is written to the Jewish people, the Hebrews. This group of Jews are considering the Law over receiving Jesus as the Messiah. In context, the above scriptures need to be understood through what Jesus has defined as sin in John 3:16–18

and again in John 16:9 (NLT), "The world's sin is that it refuses to believe in me."

This group of Jews are the first generation after the resurrection of Jesus and are in the process of being delivered from the Law of Moses, which is the covenant that God made with the Jewish people. Changing their belief system of atonement for sins was a very big deal, as one could imagine. Their temptation was staying with the Law as a foundation for the sacrifice for sins, which is what they grew up with and believed. The author, Paul, is stating that the Law offers no sacrifice for sins any longer. Jesus the Messiah is now the only sacrifice that atones for sin.

In Hebrews 10:26, by Jesus's definition of sin, deliberately continuing to sin is continuing not to believe in Jesus as the Messiah and continuing in the Law of Moses.

Scenario 7—What about one's name being erased from the Book of Life?

> All who are victorious will be clothed in white.
> I will never erase their names from the Book of
> Life, but I will announce before my Father and
> his angels that they are mine. (Rev. 3:5, NLT)

To come to a conclusion in this scenario, we need to look at the beginning and walk through one's life.

> Before I formed you in the womb I knew you;
> Before you were born I sanctified you; I ordained
> you a prophet to the nations. (Jer. 1:5, NKJV)

At the moment Jesus creates the spirit life of a person, in heaven the Lord names that person. Our God is a god of perfect order. That name is recorded in the Book of Life forever if they believe in Jesus. This is implied when Jesus stated, "I will never erase their names." Their names were recorded from their inception.

> The earth is the Lord's, and everything in it.

FATHER GOD, AFTER BELIEVING IN JESUS AS SAVIOR, CAN ONE LOSE THEIR SALVATION?

> The world and all its people belong to him.
> (Ps. 24:1, NLT)

Our names remain in the Book of Life forever if we believe in Jesus. The moment a last breath is taken without believing in Jesus is the moment that person's name is erased from the Book of Life. To complete this scenario, the entire letter to the church at Sardis needs to be brought into complete context.

> Write this letter to the angel of the church in Sardis. This is the message from the one who has the sevenfold Spirit of God and the seven stars:
>
> "I know all the things you do, and that you have a reputation for being alive—but you are dead. Wake up! Strengthen what little remains, for even what is left is almost dead. I find that your actions do not meet the requirements of my God. Go back to what you heard and believed at first; hold to it firmly. Repent and turn to me again. If you don't wake up, I will come to you suddenly, as unexpected as a thief.
>
> "Yet there are some in the church in Sardis who have not soiled their clothes with evil. They will walk with me in white, for they are worthy. 5 All who are victorious will be clothed in white. I will never erase their names from the Book of Life, but I will announce before my Father and his angels that they are mine.
>
> "Anyone with ears to hear must listen to the Spirit and understand what he is saying to the churches." (Rev. 3:1–6, NLT)

Jesus determined in John 3:16–18 who is going to heaven by whether one believes in Jesus or not. He also determined if there was any judgement for anyone who believes, which there is no judgement.

In John 16:9 Jesus states His definition of sin again as not believing in Jesus, so His negative statements cannot be for those who believe in Him. They come from two possible sources that have infiltrated the church: The first type are the enlightened ones as expressed in Hebrews 6 (above). They have a head knowledge of Jesus but have not believed in Him as Savior; they are also doing works that are not of divine nature but influencing the church by the lust of the flesh with a knowledge of the power of Jesus's name.

To clarify this group,

> Not everyone who calls out to me, "Lord! Lord!" will enter the Kingdom of Heaven. Only those who actually do the will of my Father in heaven will enter. On judgment day many will say to me, "Lord! Lord! We prophesied in your name and cast out demons in your name and performed many miracles in your name." But I will reply, "I never knew you. Get away from me, you who break God's laws." (Matt. 7:21–23, NLT).

What is breaking God's law or not meeting God's requirement under the New Covenant? Not believing in Jesus as the Son of God. *What is the will of the Father?*

> Jesus told them, "This is the only work God wants from you: Believe in the one he has sent." (John 6:29, NLT)

> Jesus came and told his disciples, "I have been given all authority in heaven and on earth. Therefore, go and make disciples of all the nations, baptizing them in the name of the Father and the Son and the Holy Spirit." (Matt 28:18–19, NLT)

*The second possible group that possibly infiltrated the church of
Sardis,*

> Dear friends, I had been eagerly planning to
> write to you about the salvation we all share. But
> now I find that I must write about something
> else, urging you to defend the faith that God has
> entrusted once for all time to his holy people. I say
> this because some ungodly people have wormed
> their way into your churches, saying that God's
> marvelous grace allows us to live immoral lives.
> The condemnation of such people was recorded
> long ago, for they have denied our only Master
> and Lord, Jesus Christ. (Jude 1:3–4, NLT)

Ultimately, for Jesus to erase the name of a born-again believer
from His Book of Life, Jesus would have to do two things: (1) what
He swore He would not do under this covenant—remember our
sins and iniquities (Psalm 103:12, NLT; Jeremiah 31:33–34, NLT;
Romans 4:4–7, NLT; Hebrews 8:12, NLT; Hebrews 10:16–17,
NLT); (2) redefine the sin that He judges to the standard of the Law
of Moses instead of simply believing in Him as Lord and Savior.

If we allow the Bible to explain itself, it will. But Scripture must
be viewed from the covenant God has with mankind since the death
and resurrection of Jesus, which is the new covenant of grace that the
apostle Paul called the Good News.

Troubled by Misunderstood Teachers

The scriptures in each scenario have brought so much torment
to my life until the Holy Spirit put my wife and me under true new
covenant-of-grace teachers. When understanding comes and scriptures like all of the above and others present themselves in stark con-
trast with the grace of God and the covenant Jesus died to give us, we
now look for what we don't understand and pursue understanding
instead of relying on how we were taught.

Side note

To clarify how my wife and I were taught, we were taught that both the old and new covenants were what God judged and governed His people with. As the scriptures stated earlier, Jesus made the Law of Moses obsolete. The Law was fulfilled when Jesus came and was crucified and raised from the dead, ending its governing authority from God's standpoint over born-again believers in Christ Jesus. The old covenant ended at the moment of Jesus's death (Hebrews 9:16–28, NLT).

> Before the way of faith in Christ was available to us, we were placed under guard by the law. We were kept in protective custody, so to speak, until the way of faith was revealed.
>
> Let me put it another way. The law was our guardian until Christ came; it protected us until we could be made right with God through faith. And now that the way of faith has come, we no longer need the law as our guardian. (Gal. 3:23–25, NLT)

Understanding what Jesus did when He made the Law of Moses obsolete for believers and understanding that the new covenant of grace alone is what God judges and governs His people by are paramount to right belief. Understanding the differences between the covenants gives one the freedom in Christ to truly be redeemed without the guilt and condemnation, which was part of the purpose of the Law of Moses, thus the apostle Paul's term of the Law as "the ministry of condemnation and death."

Here is where some of the confusion lies in discerning the covenants for believers:

> "And I will forgive their wickedness, and I will never again remember their sins."

FATHER GOD, AFTER BELIEVING IN JESUS AS SAVIOR, CAN ONE LOSE THEIR SALVATION?

> When God speaks of a "new" covenant, it means he has made the first one obsolete. It is now out of date and will soon disappear. (Heb. 8:12–13, NLT)

"Will soon disappear" leads some to think the Law is in effect. The Law of Moses is still in effect but not to govern or judge born-again believers. When Jesus returns, the Law will completely be obsolete, and the new covenant will stand alone and forevermore. Let's look at this:

> But we know that the law is good if one uses it lawfully, knowing this: that the law is not made for a righteous person, but for the lawless and insubordinate, for the ungodly and for sinners, for the unholy and profane, for murderers of fathers and murderers of mothers, for manslayers, for fornicators, for sodomites, for kidnappers, for liars, for perjurers, and if there is any other thing that is contrary to sound doctrine, according to the glorious gospel of the blessed God which was committed to my trust. (1 Tim. 1:8–11, NKJV)

Verse 9 states that the Law is not for the righteous. We believers are the righteousness of God in Christ Jesus; therefore, the Law is not our means of judgement or our means of guidance. That job now belongs to the promise of the new covenant, the Holy Spirit.

According to the apostle Paul, there is a distinct separation of covenants, and they are not to be mixed. The Law was also written on every heart so all will know right from wrong according to the purpose of the Law.

> And we have such trust through Christ toward God. Not that we are sufficient of ourselves to think of anything as being from ourselves, but our sufficiency is from God, who also made us sufficient as ministers of the new covenant, not

of the letter but of the Spirit; for the letter kills, but the Spirit gives life.

But if the ministry of death, written and engraved on stones, was glorious, so that the children of Israel could not look steadily at the face of Moses because of the glory of his countenance, which glory was passing away, how will the ministry of the Spirit not be more glorious? For if the ministry of condemnation had glory, the ministry of righteousness exceeds much more in glory. For even what was made glorious had no glory in this respect, because of the glory that excels. For if what is passing away was glorious, what remains is much more glorious. (2 Cor. 3:4–11, NKJV)

Clearly there are two entirely different covenants—one is of life while one is of condemnation and death. One covenant was signed in the blood of bulls and goats; the other was signed in the blood of the Son of the Living God by the Son of God Himself. The only thing they have in common is a holy God who wrote them both. In fact, the Law of Moses (old covenant) was made with the Jews alone; the new covenant was made for the Jews and Gentiles. The Gentiles were never included in the covenant God made through Moses at the time of its writing.

When the Gentiles sin, they will be destroyed, even though they never had God's written law. And the Jews, who do have God's law, will be judged by that law when they fail to obey it. (Rom. 2:12, NLT)

How can one discern if a pastor believes that God is governing and judging His people from both the Law of Moses and the new covenant of grace?

When one walks out of a service hearing a mixture of covenants, one will feel worse than before the service began. Feelings of guilt, condemnation, and shame are common. Paul says that a preaching-teaching mixture of covenants brings a curse to that preacher/teacher (Galatians 6–9, NKJV [below]). So what is Paul's gospel of grace? The gospel according to Paul (who wrote two-thirds of the new covenant) is this: Jesus Christ is the Son of the Living God who was beaten and crucified for the sins and the healing of the world He crated and who rose from the dead to be the once-and-for-all-time sacrifice for sins. Simple, isn't it? But it is easier to believe in a Law that requires no faith but obedience rather than to believe that the God of all creation would send His one and only Son to redeem (buy back) all mankind back to Himself by Jesus's death on the cross and His subsequent resurrection.

No Guilt, Condemnation, or Shame—Nothing but a Clean Conscience from Grace

> For the law, having a shadow of the good things to come, and not the very image of the things, can never with these same sacrifices, which they offer continually year by year, make those who approach perfect. For then would they not have ceased to be offered? For the worshipers, once purified, would have had no more consciousness of sins. But in those sacrifices there is a reminder of sins every year. For it is not possible that the blood of bulls and goats could take away sins. (Heb. 10:1–4, NKJV)

If one walks out of a service with a guilty conscience, know that Jesus paid the price for a clear, clean conscience, no matter the circumstances. Jesus doesn't want anyone thinking about the sins He paid a high price for, for one not to have to remember them. He wants all our attention.

My wife and I lived under the misconception that both covenants were in effect for believers until God delivered us into His marvelous grace. The devil has been deceiving humanity for a very long time. We were no different, and pastors who believe that way are no different. If the devil can keep one under the Law, he keeps one under the condemnation and guilt that Paul spoke of when he called the Law of Moses and the Ten Commandments the ministry of condemnation and death.

> But those who depend on the law to make them right with God are under his curse, for the Scriptures say, "Cursed is everyone who does not observe and obey all the commands that are written in God's Book of the Law." So it is clear that no one can be made right with God by trying to keep the law. For the Scriptures say, "It is through faith that a righteous person has life." This way of faith is very different from the way of law, which says, "It is through obeying the law that a person has life."
>
> But Christ has rescued us from the curse pronounced by the law. When he was hung on the cross, he took upon himself the curse for our wrongdoing. For it is written in the Scriptures, "Cursed is everyone who is hung on a tree." Through Christ Jesus, God has blessed the Gentiles with the same blessing he promised to Abraham, so that we who are believers might receive the promised Holy Spirit through faith. (Gal. 3:10–14, NLT)

I suspect the same pastors who preach both covenants ruling over God's people will vehemently disagree with the findings of this document.

To them, I would strongly encourage to read how vehemently the apostle Paul apposes anyone who believes and teaches that way:

> I marvel that you are turning away so soon from Him who called you in the grace of Christ, to a different gospel, which is not another; but there are some who trouble you and want to pervert the gospel of Christ. But even if we, or an angel

from heaven, preach any other gospel to you
than what we have preached to you, let him be
accursed. As we have said before, so now I say
again, if anyone preaches any other gospel to you
than what you have received, let him be accursed.
(Gal. 1:6–9, NKJV)

Any time the Bible repeats a word or scripture, it is a very major
point of emphasis. Just so there is no confusion about what Paul is
referring to,

Then after a period of fourteen years I again went
up to Jerusalem, [this time] with Barnabas, taking
Titus along also. I went up [to Jerusalem] because
of a [divine] revelation, and I put before them
the gospel which I preach among the Gentiles.
But I did so in private before those of reputa-
tion, for fear that I might be running or had run
[the course of my ministry] in vain. But [all went
well, for] not even Titus, who was with me, was
compelled [as some had anticipated] to be cir-
cumcised, despite the fact that he was a Greek.
My concern was because of the false brothers
[those people masquerading as Christians] who
had been secretly smuggled in [to the community
of believers]. They had slipped in to spy on the
freedom which we have in Christ Jesus, in order
to bring us back into bondage [under the Law of
Moses]. But we did not yield to them even for a
moment, so that the truth of the gospel would
continue to remain with you [in its purity]. (Gal.
2:1–5, AMP)

So Christ has truly set us free. Now make sure
that you stay free, and don't get tied up again in
slavery to the law. (Gal. 5:1, NLT)

At this point, I would like to solidify what Jesus brought and what He didn't bring:

> For the law was given by Moses, but grace and truth came by Jesus Christ. (John 1:17, KJV)

Conclusion

However, those the Father has given me will come to me, and I will never reject them. For I have come down from heaven to do the will of God who sent me, not to do my own will. 39 And this is the will of God, that I should not lose even one of all those he has given me, but that I should raise them up at the last day. For it is my Father's will that all who see his Son and believe in him should have eternal life. I will raise them up at the last day. (John 6:37–40, NLT)

In John 6:47 (NLT) Jesus also said,

"I tell you the truth, anyone who believes has eternal life. Yes, I am the bread of life!"

The Spirit alone gives eternal life. Human effort accomplishes nothing. And the very words I have spoken to you are spirit and life. (John 6:63, NLT)

When the Holy Spirit gives life, no man can destroy that life. That person cannot change their eternal direction after being born again, even though that person may not fulfill the purpose that God planned for his or her life.

So can you lose your salvation? If your answer is still yes, Mr. Tolstoy was right. I would encourage you to ask God to take you to teachers who know and understand the covenant Jesus our Lord died to give us.

Know this for sure: the only practical application of the scriptures is from and by the grace of God through Jesus Christ and Their new covenant. This covenant is not a covenant that we (humanity) have with Abba Father, King Jesus, and the Holy Spirit; it is a covenant that They have made for us.

> They serve in a system of worship that is only a copy, a shadow of the real one in heaven. For when Moses was getting ready to build the Tabernacle, God gave him this warning: "Be sure that you make everything according to the pattern I have shown you here on the mountain."
>
> But now Jesus, our High Priest, has been given a ministry that is far superior to the old priesthood, for he is the one who mediates for us a far better covenant with God, based on better promises.
>
> If the first covenant had been faultless, there would have been no need for a second covenant to replace it. (Heb. 8:5–7, NLT)

Final Thought

> If you declare with your mouth, "Jesus is Lord,"
> and believe in your heart that God raised him
> from the dead, you will be saved. For it is with
> your heart that you believe and are justified, and it
> is with your mouth that you profess your faith and
> are saved. As Scripture says, "Anyone who believes
> in him will never be put to shame." For there is
> no difference between Jew and Gentile—the same
> Lord is Lord of all and richly blesses all who call on
> him, for, "Everyone who calls on the name of the
> Lord will be saved." (Rom. 10:9–13, NLT)

> God saved you by his grace when you believed.
> And you can't take credit for this; it is a gift from
> God. Salvation is not a reward for the good things
> we have done, so none of us can boast about it.
> (Eph. 2:8–9, NLT)

What God gives a gift, He never takes back. Once you're a child of God, you're a child of God forever. He made sure of that.

The verses above say it all, and there are no conditions or exceptions attached to the new covenant once one believes in Jesus.

According to the Word of God, there is only one way to lose one's salvation:

> For if you are trying to make yourselves right
> with God by keeping the law, you have been cut
> off from Christ! You have fallen away from God's
> grace. (Gal. 5:4, NLT)

CPSIA information can be obtained
at www.ICGtesting.com
Printed in the USA
LVHW101726101122
732861LV00023B/216

9 781098 036